BUFFALO SOLDIERS WEST

BY JOHN M. CARROLL

405 Link Lane

Fort Collins, Colorado 80521

This amazing collection of pictures had its origin in, of all places, the Job Corps Training Center at Edison, New Jersey. I worked at old Camp Kilmer in this great undertaking for four years, first as a teacher and then as a teaching supervisor.

The Job Corps had a unique student population, students ranging in age from 16 to 21. In my classes throughout the four years about 80% of my students were black. Most students had reading difficulties, and it was not unusual for me to have in one class reading skills ranging from non-reader to college level. The problem was simply one of educational materials suitable for all students on all levels. Exhaustive investigation of all the publishers did not bring forth any simple solution for me either. The materials available just did not satisfy all needs. Besides having to be sensitive to ethnic differences within the classroom, my teachers and I had to walk on thin ice because of the age differences and the require-ments demanded by these differences.

The solution came to me one evening at home: Devise your own materials. I did. They liked them, black and white both. What began as a simple collection of pictures - mostly Remingtons - ended up this year in the publication of my new book, THE BLACK MILITARY EXPERIENCE IN WESTERN AMERICA, published by Liveright Publishing Corporation. Of course, what had begun as assembled facts and pictures by then had de-veloped into an anthology with numerous pictures, many of which were commissioned especially for the book. The publication of this booklet includes all of these as well as those which did not make it into the book because of editing.

I was pleased when Old Army Press agreed to pub-lish a booklet of only the pictures. I have added cap-tions to these, and can only hope the viewer of this booklet today is as enthusiastic about the particular segment of our history covered by the pictures as were my students at Job Corps.

JOHN M. CARROLL
New Brunswick, New Jersey
September 1971

dedication

THIS BOOK IS DEDICATED TO THE MEMORY
OF THE LATE JIM SKELTON, A BLACK FRIEND
AND A GREAT TEACHER FROM WHOM WE ALL
LEARNED.

LORENCE BJORKLUND

This famous illustrator of over 300 books, both adult and juvenile, lives in Croton Falls, New York. He was born in Minnesota but spent most of his adult life in the New York area where he began to build a reputation as an illustrator of the western scene by supplying drawings for the popular western pulps of the 1930's and 1940's. His reputation as an illustrator peaked with the publication of his book, FACES OF THE FRONTIER, in 1967. This was followed by THE BISON: THE GREAT AMERICAN BUFFALO in 1970. Today he is busy writing and illustrating a new book with his subject being the American Indian. I am delighted to call him a friend.

BILL CHAPPELL

I have been aware of Bill Chappell's work for several years but it was not until last year I first made contact with him at his home in Alamosa, Colorado. Having admired his art - which always appeared to me to be so very accurate - I wrote him and told him how much I appreciated what he did on canvas. His Christmas cards are a joy to behold. Although we have never met it is just a matter of time before we do, for it will be my pleasure to someday drop by and pay my respects in person.

HAROLD BUGBEE

The late Harold Dow Bugbee was born in Lexington, Massachusetts, in 1900, but he and his parents moved to Texas in 1913, bought land near Clarendon, and settled down to a quiet western life. His formal education, for the most part, transpired in Texas; he is an honored graduate of Texas A & M College. His artistic talents were combined with a sincere desire to "know the west" vicariously through a relationship with the old-timers, and an inquisitive eye for detail. One "old-timer" from whom he learned so much was Colonel Charles Goodnight. The illustrations of this fine artist have graced the pages of numerous books - most of which were published by the various presses in Texas. Even though I am a native Texan, I never knew him, and that is my loss.

JOSE CISNEROS

This great artist was born in Durango in 1910, moved to El Paso in 1927, gained his citizenship in 1948, and in the meantime built a reputation unbeatable today. He is, without a doubt, one of the most accomplished artist-historians practicing in America today. The work he has done for publications in the southwest has been unanimously acclaimed as fine works of art and are eagerly bought by collectors. We've never met, yet we count ourselves as good friends. I treasure his letters as evidence of his friendship - and as pieces of art.

NICK EGGENHOFER

This grand old gentleman can rightfully be hailed as the unofficial Dean of Western Illustrators. He was born in Germany in 1897 and came to this country in 1913. His fantastic career as an illustrator began with the western pulps in 1920 and his drawings - estimated at between 15 and 20,000 - graced almost every issue of dozens of these pulps from 1920 to 1949. His book and book jacket illustrations extended his career by many years, for they were of museum quality and greatly appreciated by publishers, authors, and collectors alike. Today, living in Cody, Wyoming, Nick is living in the third stage of his career - that which I identify as his fine art period. While here he wrote and published the definitive book on western modes of travel, WAGON, MULES AND MEN, a book which will stand as a reference for many years to come. I am very lucky to be able to call him and his wife my good friends. We have exchanged many visits and are in frequent mail and telephone contact. Nick is the subject of a three volume work now being prepared by me.

JOE GRANDEE

Joe, his wife Murlene, and I are all about the same age. Because of this we are able to communicate very freely. I had been an admirer of Joe's work for a long time, but it was not until last year we finally met. It was an instantaneous friendship which I respect and honor. Joe has recently opened a gallery near his home in Arlington, Texas, to display his incredible collection of western Americana and militariana. He is expert in the knowledge of accouterments and can be counted on to exhibit his knowledge in his outstanding art.

CHUCK KEMPER

Chuck and I have never met, yet I've been in Phoenix and Scottsdale, Arizona, several times. He did execute a series of paintings for a series of short stories on the Negro in America which I wrote for public school use and which will be published in the near future. His book illustrations have been few in number but are of the highest quality. His contribution of the picture of the court martial of Lt. Flipper was his only effort for my collection because of prior commitments. I hope the future will bring us an opportunity to work in concert professionally once again.

J. K. RALSTON

Ken and his wife have been my friends for a long time now, and it is my everlasting pleasure to have sat in his studio in Billings, Montana, and listened to him spin his tales of the old west - tales which are told with all the voice of authority. He lived most of that history himself.

An authority on Lewis & Clark and the Custer fight, Ken has succeeded in capturing most of these histories on canvas - a task only surpassed by the massive production of Charles Russell and his representation of the Lewis & Clark saga. It was only natural that I should have turned to him for the depiction of the valiant fight by Dorman at the Little Big Horn. He did not disappoint me.

STANLEY M. LONG

Stanley is a native of San Carlos, California, and was one of the first to respond to my requests for illustrations on this subject. We have never met, yet it seems as if we've been friends for years. The Christmas cards designed by him have long been admired by me, and as with Bill Chappell, this was the common strand which brought us together professionally.

FREDERIC REMINGTON

What more can be said of this giant of western art? Some fail to remember that he was a working reporter with pen and paper his camera. All of the work of his represented in this collection was done in the field and are but line drawings. His most popularly remembered canvases are the large oils hanging in museums and private collections around the world, but to me, the most exciting things he had done are represented here. Along with Charles Russell, Frederic Remington will be remembered as a true art historian - a painter of his time.

ACE POWELL

Ace is probably one of the very few living painters that can honestly be called a cowboy artist. This is different from an artist who paints cowboys. Ace is a new friend for me and my one visit to his home in Kalispell, Montana this summer cemented it for me. Unimpressed with trends or immediate rewards, Ace continues to do what he does best: paint the cowboy-western-Indian scene. As a working cowboy himself, his work can be depended upon to contain the honesty that is required of great art.

WILLIAM REUSSWIG

Although Bill lives almost in my "backyard," we've never met. I had long admired his illustrations appearing in the popular periodicals of our day, but it wasn't until his remarkable book which he wrote and illustrated, A PICTURE REPORT OF THE CUSTER FIGHT, that I contacted him. Since that initial letter I have had the pleasure of discovering his excellent work in other books, and also of discovering that Martha Sawyers - an artist of brilliance - was his wife. His work can be seen at Gallery 85 in Billings, Montana, and at the Grand Central Gallery in New York.

PAUL ROSSI

A friend of long standing, Paul wears two masks. One is as the director of one of America's most prestigious western art and history museums, the Gilcrease Institute of Tulsa, Oklahoma. The other mask is as an accomplished artist and sculptor. When I received Paul's permission to utilize his drawings from the Gilcrease's publication, "The American Scene," I knew at once my collection could be considered complete. Paul is an exceptional historian - one who researches faithfully and diligently. It shows in his work. There can be only one other fan of his more ardent in praise than I - his lovely wife, Florence, herself an accomplished writer.

the illustrations

the illustrations

BUFFALO SOLDIERS WEST

ARTIST: *Jose Cisneros*
SUBJECT:
Estevan de Dorantes
   (author's collection)

One of the first black men of major im-
portance in American history was Estavan
de Dorantes who was shipwrecked on the
Texas Coast along with his master and
Cabeza de Vaca. They wandered for years
- living with various Indian tribes - before
eventually finding their own people in
northern Mexico. He later lost his life
while leading an expedition in search of the
fabled Seven Cities of Gold.

J. CISNEROS

ARTIST: *Jose Cisneros*
SUBJECT:
Pohe-yemo's Representative
(author's collection)

The giant "black man with yellow eyes" figured very prominently in the great Pueblo Uprising in New Mexico. His origin has never been fully explained, but his presence was fully felt. His influence over the Pueblo Indians was so strong that it took an enormous military effort to break the back of the uprising and to restore peace to that part of the country once more.

ARTIST: *Jose Cisneros*
SUBJECT:
De Vargas' Drummer
    (author's collection)

During the early Spanish domination of Mexico and the southwestern part of North America, no military governor was complete without a uniformed militia - and no militia was complete without a drummer. De Vargas' drummer was from Angola.

ARTIST: Lorence Bjorklund
SUBJECT:
York
   (author's collection)

York, the servant to Captain Clark, accompanied his master on the famous Louis & Clark expedition which explored and opened the vast northwest. His services and his uniqueness in color helped immeasurably in the success of this great adventure. He was also a great favorite with the Indians who came out in great numbers just to see the "black white man."

L. Bjorklund.

ARTIST: *Jose Cisneros*
SUBJECT:
Mounted Black Cavalryman on Guard Duty
    (author's collection)

Actual combat between Indians and the military in the southwest was rare. Most of the time was spent in endless patrols, constant vigilance, and frequent guard duty. Whenever anything transpired to break this boredom - a dance, games, a hunt, or even chase and combat - it was entered into with tremendous relish and vigor.

ARTIST: *Jose Cisneros*
SUBJECT:
Lt. Henry Ossian Flipper
    (author's collection)

When this first black graduate of West Point assumed his first duties in Indian Territory he was the subject of much discussion: praise as well as criticism. Even though his service career was short - called to a halt by a very much disputed court martial charge - he continued to serve his country in many ways. Among his accomplishments which can be considered firsts was his fantastic efforts in translating all the old Spanish Land Grants from the original language into English. This feat enabled legal jurisdictions of all disputed lands to be resolved much more quickly than could have been imagined.

ARTIST: *Chuck Kemper*
SUBJECT:
Court Martial of Lt. Flipper
  (author's collection)

The first black graduate of the United States Military Academy received a court martial at Fort Davis, Texas, for alleged misuse of military funds. Many believe that the charges were falsified by the commanding officer. Review of his trial today would indicate this was the case.

C. Kemper

ARTIST: Stanley M. Long
SUBJECT: Battle of Florida Mountains
              (author's collection)

"Corporal Clifton Greaves fought like a cornered lion and managed to shoot and bask a gap through the swarm of Apaches." For his bravery in action, the gallant corporal was awarded the Medal of Honor.

ARTIST: Stanley M. Long
SUBJECT: Battle of Gavilan Canyon
          (author's collection)

"Sergeant Brent Woods came to the succor of his wounded comrades and finally drove Nana's band of Apache across the Mexican border." So read the citation when this brave cavalryman earned his Medal of Honor.

ARTIST: Stanley M. Long
SUBJECT: Battle of Kickapoo Springs
        (author's collection)

"Sergeant Emanuel Stance charged the Indians and once more managed to rout the enemy, this since capturing five more horses." Sergeant Stance was awarded his Medal of Honor for his heroic action against the Indians during the campaigns in the southwest.

"*Sergeant Boyne flanked the small attacking party and charged them with such ferocity that they were driven off.*" *Sergeant Thomas Boyne was awarded his Medal of Honor as a result of this heroic action.*

Sergeant John Denny, 9th U. S. Cavalry, was awarded the Medal of Honor for his exceptional bravery - without thought of safety for his own life - when removing a wounded comrade to a place of safety during an engagement against the Apache Indians in Los Animas Canyon.

ARTIST: Jose Cisneros
SUBJECT:
Battle on Pecos River
    (author's collection)

Private Pompey Factor, Trumpeter Isaac Payne, and Sergeant John Ward - all Seminole-Negro Scouts on duty with the 24th Infantry - were conspicuously heroic in an engagement against Kiowas and Comanches on the Pecos River. Their actions won them praise and the Medal of Honor.

ARTIST: *Nick Eggenhofer*
SUBJECT:
A 9th U. S. Cavalryman
(author's collection)

Ever vigilant, the trooper, whether on scout
or on guard, had the safety of his command
in his hands.

ARTIST: *Jose Cisneros*
SUBJECT:
The Battle of Fort Tulerosa
    (author's collection)

Sergeant George Jordan, 9th U. S. Cavalry, was awarded the Medal of Honor for his bravery in action in two battles in New Mexico: the Battle of Fort Tulerosa and the Battle of Carrizo Canyon. His quick thinking and instant reflexes prevented a possible slaughter at Fort Tulerosa - even though he was greatly outnumbered. The superb discipline and dedication to duty possessed by him and his very small detachment would have been victorious anywhere.

ARTIST: *Jose Cisneros*
SUBJECT:
Fort Quitman
  (author's collection)

Of all the frontier military posts in the Trans-Pecos area, probably the least popular was Fort Quitman. It was a primitive existence but one which the black units accepted with little complaint and always with respect for military authority and duty. Even though this fort was isolated and unpleasant, its existence helped bring to an end the infamous raids of the Apache chieftain, Victorio.

ARTIST: *Jose Cisneros*
SUBJECT:
The Seminole-Negro Indian Scouts
    (author's collection)

This small detachment of men were sworn into military service as scouts for the military forces of the United States stationed in the southwest. They were of mixed parentage but of a single loyalty - a loyalty that was not returned in kind.

Lt. Nolan's lost patrol of the 10th Cavalry unit on the Staked Plains of Texas resulted in a staggering display of perserverance as the troopers went 86 hours without water and sometimes drank the blood of their horses to prevent dehydration and certain death.

ARTIST: Jose Cisneros
SUBJECT:
The "Other Side" Of Military Life On The Frontier   *(author's collection)*

Service on the southwestern frontier was not always accompanied by sun and wind and sand.   When it rained it poured, but assigned duties prevailed no matter what the weather.   It was tedious, boring, and uncomfortable with little rewards for doing it.

ARTIST: Ace Powell
SUBJECT: Mounted Action at the Wham Paymaster Robbery
(author's collection)

Although the robbery of the military payroll in Arizona Territory has never been solved, the dedication of the black soldiers in attempting to save the payroll won praise. The bandits did not take the payroll easily.

Sergeant Benjamin Brown and Corporal Isaiah Mays of the Twenty-fourth Infantry, each won a Medal of Honor for heroic action in attempting unsuccessfully to save the military payroll from a gang of highwaymen near Yuma, Arizona Territory. This robbery is still unsolved.

ARTIST: Ace Powell
SUBJECT: Action at the Wham Paymaster Robbery
           (author's collection)

Personal bravery in the face of overwhelming odds - complicated by a surprise action - only intensified the drama of this daring robbery in Arizona Territory.

© Paul A Rossi 69

If an outfit had a particularly strong "spit-and-polish" commandant, one way to relieve boredom on the frontier was to have frequent dress parades and formal Retreat ceremonies. This kept the soldier alert to his own position and competition between units was keen. Even though they must have grumbled at the frequency of these events, the discipline involved served them well when it came to the more strenuous duties on the frontier.

ARTIST: Harold Bugbee
SUBJECT: *Black Trooper On The Texas Frontier*
          (courtesy Houston Harte)

The black troopers faced extraordinary dangers on our western frontiers - and no more so than during the Apache Indian Wars. To be cut off from the main body of troopers often resulted in death. The trooper had to be quick and know when to run and when to fight.

ARTIST: *Jose Cisneros*
SUBJECT:
The Battle of Carrizo Canyon
   (author's collection)

Sergeant Thomas Shaw was awarded the Medal of Honor for exceptional bravery in action in the famed Battle of Carrizo Canyon. It was his cool action and initiative which helped decide the victory that day.

ARTIST: Jose Cisneros
SUBJECT:
The Battle of Canyon Blanco
    (author's collection)

"For bravery and invaluable service to the commanding officer at the Battle of Canyon Blanco," was how his citation read. His conspicuous bravery was but second nature to this member of an almost but forgotten group of people. Private Adam Paine was but one of several Seminole-Negro Scouts on duty with the U. S. military forces during the Apache Campaigns. He proudly wore his Medal of Honor on his "uniform."

ARTIST: *Frederic Remington*
SUBJECT:
Trooper With Equipment - At Ease

Rest came frequently when in the field. This was necessary to feed and water mounts as well as to give them a proper rest. All this came before the trooper could rest. The logistics of maintaining the cavalry in the field during a campaign in the southwest were overwhelming and often were directly responsible for the prolongation of the campaign. The task of mobility and of having food and water for man and horse at specified junctions would often signal the end of a chase. The Indians knew this problem existed with the cavalry and always played it to the best of their ability. These were incredible hardships not often thought of by the casual student of history.

ARTIST: *Frederic Remington*
SUBJECT:
A Pull At The Canteen

*When in the desert water was always the
most precious mineral. No one knew this
any better than the trooper who had to
serve in this kind of environment. Very
often the trooper would share his last drop
of water with his mount for he knew only
too well that without water and horse he
had little chance for survival.*

ARTIST: *Frederic Remington*
SUBJECT:
A Study of Action

Each trooper in the cavalry had to be a skilled horseman. This talent was never more needed than in the difficult terrain of the southwest druing the Geronimo campaign. The 10th U. S. Cavalry was often faced with all but impossible trails to follow. They frequently had to blaze their own way.

ARTIST: Joe Grandee
SUBJECT: *Cavalrymen in Dismounted Action*
          (courtesy the artist)

A small group of troopers sometimes had to make a stand against Indians in a surprise attack and dismounted.
In a few cases this was a "last stand," because of being tremendously outnumbered. Their expert marks-
manship, however, made the enemy pay dearly for their lives.

ARTIST: Joe Grandee
SUBJECT:
Mounted Tenth Cavalryman
    (author's collection)

The trooper on all the western frontiers had to be alert at all times. Not only did he have to be an excellent horseman, he had to be a crack shot as well. His uniform worn on the frontier would have elicited serious condemnation from the military purists in the east, but a knife at his side often meant the difference between life and death, military regulations notwithstanding. His variations of uniform were intended to meet the existing conditions. All in all, the frontier soldier was pretty self-sufficient.

ARTIST: *Lorence Bjorklund*
SUBJECT:
Escort Duty In The Northwest
    (author's collection)

One of the most tedious duties anywhere on the frontier was escort duty. The pioneers moved slowly and frequently rested several days at a time. The cavalryman was forced to move at that pace as well. However, without their protection many of the pioneers would never have made it across this continent.

ARTIST: *Jose Cisneros*
SUBJECT:
In The Field At Wintertime
(author's collection)

The cumbersome uniforms necessary for warmth did not in any way prevent action in the field even on the coldest days. This trooper tied his scarf around his head in order to protect his ears from the cold - and that was all the protection from exposure to the elements he had other than his regulation uniform. Duty at this time of the year was difficult and dangerous because of the natural elements and not the enemy.

ARTIST: *Jose Cisneros*
SUBJECT:
The Battle of Milk River
   (author's collection)

Sergeant Henry Johnson was cited for bravery in action during the Battle of Milk River in Colorado and was awarded the Medal of Honor. He was with Captain Dodge's unit, Troop D, 9th U. S. Cavalry, when they came to the rescue of Major Thornburgh, besieged by the Utes. Sergeant Johnson imperiled his own life on numerous occasions when he crawled to the only source of water and obtained that life-sustaining liquid for his wounded comrades.

ARTIST: J. K. Ralston
SUBJECT: *Isaiah Dorman at the Little Big Horn*
           (author's collection)

Isaiah Dorman was the only black man on the famous Sioux Expedition of 1876 and at the Battle of the Little Big Horn. He lost his life in that famous battle even though he was known by the Sioux as the husband of a Sioux woman. It is believed, therefore, that he was killed by Cheyenne Indians.

ARTIST: Lorence Bjorklund
SUBJECT:
The Johnson County War
    (author's collection)

The military frequently had to function as frontier police. The Johnson County War of Wyoming was but one incident. It was the duty of three companies of the 9th U. S. Cavalry to bring and maintain peace to this part of Wyoming - a task which they performed most admirably under very difficult conditions.

ARTIST: Lorence Bjorklund
SUBJECT: The Battle of Clay Creek Mission
          (author's collection)

Corporal William O. Wilson, Troop I, 9th U. S. Cavalry, was awarded the Medal of Honor for his participation in this battle which took place on 30 December 1890 shortly after the infamous Massacre at Wounded Knee Creek, Dakota Territory (now South Dakota).

ARTIST: *Paul Rossi*
SUBJECT:
A Ninth Cavalryman
 (courtesy the artist)

At first most of the troopers in this newly organized command could not read or write. Their desire to improve their lot and to make a success of their own unit resulted in many of them going to school on off-duty hours. Not only did this improve their commands it improved their attitudes toward themselves and toward each other.

ARTIST: *Paul Rossi*
SUBJECT
Trooper in Casual Uniform
   (courtesy the artist)

*Service in the southwest - with all its heat
and boredom - could break even the best
of soldiers. But it could not harm the man
with a sense of humor.*

ARTIST: *Paul Rossi*
SUBJECT:
Study of Ninth Cavalryman In Dress
Uniform   (courtesy the artist)

Although the dress uniforms of the day were stiff, hot and sometimes clumsy, it did not matter much when it came to the aspect of competition. Awareness of himself and intense pride in his company replaced all other considerations.

ARTIST: *Paul Rossi*
SUBJECT:
Tenth Cavalry Types
    (courtesy the artist)

It took rugged men to survive on the frontier, but even the most rugged often had a sense of humor. Sometimes they would decorate their military uniforms with feathers and flowers just for the fun of it. Life was simple then and pleasures were few and far between.

ARTIST: *Bill Chappell*
SUBJECT: *On The Trail To Carrizal, Mexico - 1916*
           (author's collection)

The problems of mobility and supply had always been the most serious constancy on the frontier. It was never more obvious than in 1916 when in the Mexican Sonoran desert on the trail to Carrizal - and destiny for the Tenth U. S. Cavalry.

[54]

ARTIST: Bill Chappell
SUBJECT: An Engagement in Mexico - 1916
                (author's collection)

The Punitive Expedition against Mexico in 1916 was but a prelude to World War I. Notwithstanding, the Fight At Carrizal was to be the most unnecessary engagement the 10th U. S. Cavalry ever had - and a costly one too.

ARTIST: Lorence Bjorklund
SUBJECT:
The Brownsville Affray
    (author's collection)

A few members of the Twenty-fifth Infantry were accused of "shooting up the town" in Brownsville, Texas, in 1906. This was a small riot with obvious racial undertones. When the subsequent investigation could not find the alleged guilty men, President Theodore Roosevelt had the entire battalion discharged from the service. This mass punishment was later declared unconstitutional and the President had to reverse his orders.

L. Bjorklund

ARTIST: *Jose Cisneros*
SUBJECT:
The Punitive Expedition of 1916
    (author's collection)

Before World War I was an actuality, the engagements against the Villa and Carranza forces in Mexico occupied much of the time of the American military forces - and commanded much space in the newspapers. Border patrol was but one of the major duties of the 10th U. S. Cavalry.

J. CISNEROS

ARTIST: Lorence Bjorklund

SUBJECT: The Punitive Expedition In Mexico - 1916
(author's collection)

Incidents all along the United States-Mexican border caused much concern in Washington. The 10th U. S. Cavalry was but one unit sent to the arena of action. Most of the duties entailed nothing much more than constant patrol.

ARTIST: *Jose Cisneros*

SUBJECT:

Trooper at Nogales - August 1918
   (author's collection)

World War I provided some long-forgotten shooting episodes in this country. German agents' activities along the border in Mexico was cause for alarm and preparedness. Nogales' main street is the border between the United States and Mexico, and although complete harmony was the general rule, August, 1918, saw the exception. A shooting episode between members of the 10th Cavalry and the 25th Infantry on our side of the border and some members of the Mexican federal garrison (goaded by German agents) was the international incident both sides would like to forget.

ARTIST: *Jose Cisneros*
SUBJECT:
On Foot in Mexico - 1916
   (author's collection)

The experiences on our border during the Punitive Expedition in Mexico in 1916 proved to be more than just an occasional armed conflict. Heat and dust were allied with the devil and were frequently responsible for unusual circumstances such as being lost in the desert, dehydration, and heat exhaustion. The regulation uniforms and equipment did not help the situation much either. However, respect for a trooper's horse was still a paramount consideration.

J. CISNEROS

ARTIST: Lorence Bjorklund
SUBJECT:
The Lost Soldier - 1916
    (author's collection)

The fighting in Mexico in 1916 produced several dramatic moments. One of the most dramatic was the Fight at Carrizal where many members of the 10th Cavalry were lost or captured. Those who managed to escape were faced with endless miles of desert and few life supports were in evidence. One who escaped and made his way back to his lines was Corporal Henry C. Houston who wrote one of the most revealing accounts of the engagement in a letter to the sister of his commanding officer, Lt. Howe. That letter was given to me by the officer (Colonel Howe) and I have given it to the Rare Documents Department of the Library at West Point.

ARTIST: Lorence Bjorklund
SUBJECT: The Yaqui Indian Fight - 1918
   (author's collection)

The last Indian fight engaged in by the 10th Cavalry was as recently as January 9, 1918. That afternoon some 30 Yaqui opened fire on Troop E of the 10th Cavalry. It was caused, primarily, by the Indians' and the white man's different interpretations of the meaning of a border. To an Indian who had lived all his life in an area free of such man-made devises, the border between the United States and Mexico was meaningless.

ARTIST: *Jose Cisneros*
SUBJECT:
A Retired Cavalryman
   (author's collection)

Once a trooper had reached the age of retirement there was little else to do but rest on his laurels and dream of glories past. Many of these men married and retired in the same area as their last assignment which in many cases was Fort Davis, Texas and Fort Huachuca, Arizona. It was an easy life but one earned after experiencing many dangers in making the frontier safe for the pioneers and early settlers.